# HOW TO USE
## LAW LIBRARY

# HOW TO USE A SCOTTISH LAW LIBRARY

## D. D. MACKEY

Librarian
Maclay Murray & Spens

Edinburgh
May 1992

First Published 1992
Reprinted 1993


© 1992
W. GREEN & SON LTD


ISBN 0 414 01026 4

A catalogue record for this book
is available from the British Library


*The moral right of the author has been asserted*


Printed by Image Press Ltd.

# PREFACE

This book is intended as a guide to using a Scottish law library and to the reference sources to be found there. It is aimed at all library users, be they practitioners, academics or students. I hope that it will also be helpful to those who may not be familiar with the Scottish legal system and the repositories of Scottish law.

I would like to thank those colleagues who assisted me by reading and commenting on the text and Maclay Murray & Spens for the use of their word processing system.

I must acknowledge the use of a number of other publications in the same field. I acknowledge in particular the origin of the format of the Appendix to this book which is taken from this book's sister publication, Dane and Thomas, *How to Use a Law Library*, 2nd ed., Sweet & Maxwell, 1987.

The responsibility for any errors or omissions rests with the author.

D. D. MACKEY
*Maclay Murray & Spens*
*3 Glenfinlas Street*
*Edinburgh*

# CONTENTS

# CHAPTER 1
# Introduction

### Development of Scots Law

Scottish law has developed as something of a hybrid system. It bears the marks of both an institutional civilian system, the strongest influences being European, particularly Dutch and French, and also of the English common law. The continental systems were drawn substantially from Roman law and these influences have been very strong in establishing an 'institutional' tradition in Scotland as compared with the common law development of England. In 1681 Lord Stair published his *Institutions of the Law of Scotland* which set out the law of the whole of Scotland at that time. This work and the others that followed are still regarded as sources of Scots law.

Scotland and England were formally joined together to form the United Kingdom of Great Britain by the Act of Union of 1707. However, express provision was made for the preservation of the existing Scottish courts and legal system and as a result Scotland still forms a separate jurisdiction with its own courts. The Act of Union also provided that for civil matters the final Court of Appeal would be the House of Lords. The supreme criminal court remains the High Court of Justiciary sitting as a court of appeal. Whilst Scotland has preserved its own legal system, the great increase, particularly in the latter part of this century, in legislation has led to the current situation where an increasing proportion of law is common to both England and Scotland. The impact of EEC legislation is also becoming steadily greater and with the harmonisation of laws required by the EEC, Scotland must keep abreast of EEC law.

It is within the areas of private and criminal law that the main differences remain.[1]

---

[1] For further reading on the development of the Scottish legal system see: Lord Cooper, *The Scottish Legal Tradition*, the Saltire Society, 1991; or D. M. Walker, *The Scottish Legal System*, W. Green, 1992. There are also two useful articles: *The Law Librarian* (the Journal of the British and Irish Association of Law Librarians), Sweet & Maxwell, August 1991.

The legal profession is divided as in England and Wales. Those who have rights of audience before the supreme courts are advocates, equivalent to barristers. All advocates are members of the Faculty of Advocates. The solicitors' profession is organised in much the same way as in England, but the Law Society of Scotland is quite separate from the English Law Society.

**Scottish Courts**

The Scottish Courts are as listed below. Civil cases are heard by the Sheriff Courts, Court of Session and House of Lords: criminal cases by the District Courts, Sheriff Courts and High Court of Justiciary. Other courts and tribunals exist for specific purposes.

Civil cases

*Sheriff Court*
This is the inferior but nonetheless important court. Scotland has six Sheriffdoms each with a Sheriff Principal. Each Sheriffdom is divided into several Sheriff Courts, there being 50 in all. Appeals from the Sheriff Court are made to the Sheriff Principal.

*Court of Session*
This is the superior civil court and sits as both a court of first instance and a court of appeal. It sits in Parliament House in Edinburgh. The Court of Session consists of both the Outer House and Inner House. The Outer House is exclusively a court of first instance. The Inner House consists of two Divisions of equal authority. The First is presided over by the Lord President, the Second by the Lord Justice Clerk. The Inner House sits mainly as a court of appeal.

*House of Lords*
This is the final court of appeal in Scottish civil cases. In modern times, two of the Law Lords are normally Scottish, however, there is no necessity that a Scottish Law Lord be on the bench during a Scottish appeal. Appeals are allowed on both fact and law although only a few Scottish cases will be heard each year.

Criminal cases

*District Court*
This court consists of a stipendiary magistrate and one or more Justices of the Peace and deals only with small cases.

*Sheriff Court*
In criminal cases there is no appeal from the Sheriff to the Sheriff Principal but only to the High Court of Justiciary. The case load is large and trials may be by jury.

*High Court of Justiciary*
This has jurisdiction over all Scotland in respect of all crimes, and acts as both a court of first instance and a court of appeal. As a court of first instance cases are held both in Edinburgh and on circuit as required. Trials are by jury and the judges are those of the Court of Session.

Others

Examples of specialist courts and tribunals are the Lands Tribunal for Scotland, Road Traffic Commissioners, Licensing Board and Industrial Tribunals.

**Scottish Law Libraries**

Scotland has a wide variety of law libraries including professional, government, academic and private libraries. The main law library in Scotland, the Advocates Library, is situated in the building of the Court of Session in Parliament Square, Edinburgh. The library has become part of the National Library of Scotland and as such now receives books on legal deposit. The National Library of Scotland is one of the few copyright libraries in Great Britain and thus is entitled to receive a free copy of every book published in Great Britain. There is no direct access to the library for individuals who are not members of the Faculty of Advocates. However, the collection is available to the general public for reference purposes through the National Library of Scotland.

Other Scottish libraries include the three others situated in Parliament Square, of which the Signet Library is the largest. The two rival professional societies of solicitors in Edinburgh, the Writers to the Signet (WS) and the Solicitors in the Supreme Courts (SSC) each have their own library. The Supreme Court's library provides a service primarily for the judges themselves.

The largest non-academic law library in Glasgow is that of the Royal Faculty of Procurators in Glasgow which has an extensive collection. Access is limited to members of the Faculty.

In Aberdeen, the largest non-academic law library is the Society of Advocates Library; access again is restricted.

The Universities of Aberdeen, Dundee, Edinburgh, Glasgow and Strathclyde each have law libraries with large collections. University libraries, although designed to serve the needs of their students/academics, will often allow access to members of the public for particular research projects.

There are various government libraries such as the library of the Scottish Law Commission, Edinburgh and the library of the Scottish Office, Edinburgh.

The legal profession in Scotland has expanded greatly in the last ten years and many of the larger Scottish legal firms now have their own libraries.

The following is a list of the main Scottish law libraries:

**Advocates Library**
Faculty of Advocates
Parliament House
Parliament Square
Edinburgh, EH1 1RP
Tel: 031 226 5071

**Glasgow District Libraries**
The Mitchell Library
North Street
Glasgow
G3 7DN
Tel: 031 221 7030

**Royal Faculty of Procurators in Glasgow**
12 Nelson Mandela Place
Glasgow G2 1BT
Tel: 041 332 3593

**Scottish Law Commission**
140 Causewayside
Edinburgh
EH9 1PR
Tel: 031 668 2131

**Signet Library**
Parliament Square
Edinburgh
EH1 1RF
Tel: 031 225 4923

**University of Aberdeen**
Taylor Law Library
Taylor Building
Aberdeen AB9 2UB
Tel: 0224 272000

**University of Dundee**
Law Library
Scrymgeour Building
Park Place
Dundee DD1 4HN
Tel: 0382 23181

**University of Edinburgh**
Law Library
Old College
South Bridge
Edinburgh EH8 9YL
Tel: 031 650 2043

**University of Glasgow**
University Library
Hillhead Street
Glasgow
G12 8QE
Tel: 041 339 8855

**University of Strathclyde**
Law Library
Stenhouse Building
173 Cathedral Street
Glasgow G4 0RG
Tel: 041 552 4400

# CHAPTER 2
# Reference Sources

The purpose of this chapter is to describe the main reference works of use in a Scottish law library. The list is not exhaustive but does cover the sources most frequently referred to throughout this book. In later chapters details will be given on how to use the works for specific research purposes.

**Current Law**

The Current Law service aims to provide a comprehensive guide and update to the law of the United Kingdom. Prior to 1991, the service was provided in two formats: *Scottish Current Law*, published by W. Green; and *Current Law*, published by Sweet & Maxwell. The Scottish Current Law service included the English and Welsh service. The Current Law service excluded all purely Scottish material. The Current Law service is now jointly published by W. Green and Sweet & Maxwell and, at the date of publication, comprises the following parts:

Current Law Monthly Digest

This covers the law of Scotland, England and Wales, Northern Ireland and EEC developments of direct impact on the law. The parts are divided alphabetically by country and within the country sections, alphabetically by subject. The Digests cover reported cases, legislation, government department circulars, books and articles. There are separate tables of quantum awards in damages cases, an alphabetical cumulative index to statutory instruments, an alphabetical cumulative index to cases, cumulative legislation citator, progress of Bills table, words and phrases table and statutory dates of commencement table. There is also a subject index at the back of each monthly part which is cumulative as are all the indexes. The indexes refer to the relevant paragraph in the *Current Law*

*Monthly Digest* in which the item is mentioned. Scottish items in the index are identified by the letter 'S' after the *Current Law* paragraph number.

### Current Law Statutes Annotated

This provides the text of all Public General Acts which are annotated by an appropriate expert. The Acts of Sederunt and Adjournal were also published as part of the Scottish Current Law Statutes Annotated service until the end of 1991.

### Case Citator

The *Case Citator* is an alphabetical index of cases covering the full name of any case reported since 1947, citations in both the law reports and journals where the case may have been digested and a judicial history of cases considered since 1947. Where a case has been subsequently reversed or applied the citator will provide a reference to the appropriate paragraph number in the *Current Law Year Book* for the year of the subsequent case. The *Scottish Current Law Case Citator* currently appears in two bound volumes for the years 1948 to 1976 and 1977 to 1988. The index to the Scottish cases is at the *back* of each volume. There is also a smaller bound volume for the years 1989 to 1991 with a separate Scottish index at the back. The case citator sections in the monthly parts from 1992 list Scottish cases within the general index of cases. Cases in the monthly parts which have been judicially considered are printed in the index in lower case type. References to cases reported in journals appear in square brackets.

### Legislation Citator

The *Legislation Citator* is a chronological list of legislation listed by year and chapter number of Act. The legislation citators appear in two bound volumes for the years 1947–1971 and 1972–1988. There is also a smaller bound volume for the years 1989 to 1991. In the bound volumes an alphabetical list of Acts appears. A list of Statutory Instruments affected during the period of the citator is also given. The citator provides details of amendments and repeals made to statutes from 1947, details of cases which consider sections of Acts which appear under the relevant section and details of Statutory Instruments issued under statutory provisions since 1947. A table of legislation not yet in force is also published and an updater. From January 1992 the *Legislation Citator* is published in the *Monthly Digest*: however, the current information on Statutory Instruments affected is not available in the monthly digest. This can only be found in the annual *Current Law Year Book* or bound *Legislation Citator*.

Current Law Year Books

The consolidated version of the *Monthly Digest* in an annual bound volume. Where a case summary has been superseded by a further report, the reference will be amended. In the bound volumes the following tables appear: table of cases, table of quantum of damages for personal injuries or death, Statutory Instruments (listed both alphabetically by subject and numerically), table of Statutory Instruments affected during the year, table of current law reports, table of abbreviations, dates of commencement of statutes, tables of books and articles published throughout the year, arranged alphabetically by subject, and an index.

**Legal Journals Index**

Published by Legal Information Resources Limited from 1986. It is published in monthly issues which are cumulated quarterly. An annual bound volume service cumulates the year. The *Index* covers all journals published in the United Kingdom which are either devoted to law or often contain articles on legal topics. The *Legal Journals Index* is available in electronic format. The bulk of the *Index* is devoted to an alphabetical subject index of articles which is quite specific. The other indexes are by author, by case discussed and by legislation discussed. There is also at present a book review index, indexing in which journals books have been reviewed. Legal Information Resources Limited will, for a fee, provide copies of the majority of items which they index.

**Daily Law Reports Index**

Published by Legal Information Resources Limited from 1988 onwards. It is published fortnightly covering reports from the previous two weeks. The fortnightly parts cumulate quarterly and there is an optional cumulative bound volume service. The service covers *The Times*, *Financial Times*, *Independent*, *Guardian*, *Scotsman* and *Lloyds List*. The information is indexed into a parties' names index, case index, subject index, legislation index (cases which consider a part of legislation), ships' names index; and in the quarterly issues a cumulative case report index which provides references to fuller reports of the case if it has subsequently been reported in any of the major law reports series.

**Index to the Statutes**

This is published annually by Her Majesty's Stationery Office,

(HMSO), in two volumes and is an alphabetically arranged subject index to legislation in force at the date of publication. The front part of Volume 1 contains useful tables of statutes covering the Acts of England, Great Britain and the United Kingdom, Acts of Scotland to 1707, Acts of Ireland to 1800 and Local and Personal Acts with a note of the subject heading under which information will be found. Notes on Scottish Acts are at the end of each subject division.

### Chronological Table of the Statutes

This is published annually by HMSO in two volumes and is a chronological table of the statutes for the period 1235 to the year of publication. It comprises four sections, the first covers the Acts of the Parliaments of England, Great Britain and the United Kingdom, the second the Acts of the Parliament of Scotland from 1424 to 1707. Acts recorded in the parliamentary proceedings prior to the reign of James I are not included (these are contained in Volume 1 of the Record Edition). The third part covers Church Assembly Measures and General Synod Measures and the fourth, local and personal Acts. The statutes are listed with notes of amendments or repeals and the affecting legislation. A note of abbreviations used is given at the front of Volume 1.

### Index to Government Orders

This is published every two years by HMSO. It is the equivalent of the *Index to the Statutes* for Statutory Instruments. The first part of Volume 1 is devoted to a chronological table of statutes with a note of the subject heading under which information will be found. The main part of the volumes is devoted to subject headings under which the statutory powers are listed. Under these the Statutory Instruments themselves are listed, alongside a note of any such exercised Statutory Instruments. A table of abbreviations used in the index is given in Volume 1.

### Table of Government Orders

This is published annually in two volumes by HMSO. This is the equivalent for Statutory Instruments of the *Chronological Table of the Statutes*. All Statutory Instruments and Statutory Rules and Orders are listed showing any amendments with details of the amending legislation.

### HMSO Daily, Weekly, Monthly and Annual Lists of Publications

These are produced by HMSO detailing government publications for the specific time period. These include parliamentary proceedings, Acts which have received Royal Assent, Statutory Instruments, Command Papers etc. and notes on agency publications. HMSO is the main UK agency for the distribution of EC publications.

## Electronic Sources

Lexis

*Lexis* is the world's largest and most comprehensive collection of up-to-date legal source materials held in electronic format. Butterworths should be contacted for subscription details. Full training on *Lexis* is offered to subscribers to the database. It is a full text database: namely, all documents, cases and legislative materials appear in full and are thus retrievable by searching for any word or combination of words which may have appeared in the original text. The database consists of several libraries. Those most frequently used in Scotland are Scots law, United Kingdom law, Commonwealth law (which allows searching through both the English and Scottish libraries simultaneously) and European Community law.

The Scots law library contains the full text of the *Session Cases* from January 1950, *Scots Law Times* from January 1950, *Scottish Criminal Case Reports* from 1981 and *Scottish Civil Law Reports* from 1986. Unreported cases of Scottish decisions in the House of Lords from July 1986, Inner House decisions from 1982 and Outer House decisions from 1985 are also included. Scottish legislation is not available on *Lexis*. Scottish provisions in UK Acts from January 1980 are included and amendments are incorporated into the original text. The full text of the *Journal of the Law Society of Scotland* from 1990 is also available in the UK Law Journals library.[1]

EEC databases

For details of EEC databases contact the European Commission Office. Examples of the EC databases available are: CELEX, which contains the text of the Official Journal; RAPID, which contains the text of EC press releases; and INFO92 which contains all the information relating to the single market legislation.

---

[1] For details of search techniques see Dane & Thomas, *How to Use a Law Library*, 2nd ed., Sweet & Maxwell, 1987.

# Chapter 3
# Textbooks and Reference Works

## Institutional Writings

The 'institutional writings', so called because many were modelled on the *Institutes* of Justinian, cover, for the most part, the whole of the law of Scotland. The authority of the institutional writer is on a par with a decision of the Inner House of the Court of Session. Where there is no law to the contrary on an express point, then any statement made in an institutional writing will almost certainly be taken as settling the law. It is important to acknowledge that it is only the particular writings outlined below which are authoritative. Other works by the same authors will not command the same authority.

The most frequently acknowledged institutional writings are as follows:

(1) Sir Thomas Craig: *Jus Feudale*, 1655.
(2) James Dalrymple, Viscount Stair: *The Institutions of the Law of Scotland*, 1681.
(3) Andrew McDougall, Lord Bankton: *An Institute of the Laws of Scotland in Civil Rights*, 1751 to 1753.
(4) Professor John Erskine: *An Institute of the Law of Scotland*, 1773.
(5) Professor George Joseph Bell: *Commentaries on the Law of Scotland and on the Principles of Mercantile Jurisprudence*, 1804; and *Principles of the Law of Scotland*, 1829.
(6) Sir A. Alison: *Principles and Practice of the Criminal Law of Scotland*, 1832.
(7) Baron David Hume: *Commentaries on the Law of Scotland Respecting Crimes*, 1797.
(8) Sir George MacKenzie: *The Laws and Customs of Scotland in Matters Criminal*, 1678.

Butterworths have reissued several of these institutional writings in their Scottish Legal Classics series.

### Encyclopaedias

When searching for information on a subject for the first time the ideal starting place is with either an encyclopaedia or a general textbook. The main reference sources are as follows.

Butterworths in conjunction with the Law Society of Scotland have published the *Stair Memorial Encyclopaedia of the Laws of Scotland* (popularly referred to as 'Stair'). The work is in 25 volumes, with a bound index volume and began publication in 1989. It incorporates references to EEC law wherever necessary and is kept up to date by a looseleaf service volume. For general areas of the law it is often a very useful starting point and for more obscure areas of the law it may be the primary source of information.

The *Encyclopaedia of the Laws of Scotland*, published by W. Green, 1949, is now rather out of date.

Information on the procedural aspects of the Scottish courts is to be found in the *Parliament House Book*, a looseleaf encyclopaedia, published by W. Green.

### Reference Books

For definitions of Scottish legal terms, refer to either A. G. M. Duncan's *Green's Glossary of Scottish Legal Terms*, 3rd ed., W. Green, 1992 or J. A. Beaton's *Scottish Legal Terms and Expressions*, W. Green, 1982. The *Stair Memorial Encyclopaedia* also provides a glossary of Scottish legal terms.

To check citations refer to D. Raistrick's *Index to Legal Citations and Abbreviations*, Professional Books, 1981. The index covers the United Kingdom, Commonwealth and several member countries of the European Community.

All law libraries will have a collection of directories. The main Scottish law directory is still that published by T. & T. Clark, commonly referred to as 'the *White Book*'. In addition to information on solicitors holding a practising certificate in Scotland, there are detailed indexes of the members of the Faculty of Advocates, tables of fees, legal aid tables and information given on various affiliated professional groups, such as banks, accountants and surveyors. Butterworths began production of a rival directory, entitled the *Blue Book*, in 1991, which provides a similar range of information.

### General Textbooks

Arguably the most widely used general student textbook is Gloag and Henderson's *Introduction to the Law of Scotland*, currently in its 9th edition, published in 1987 by W. Green. Coverage is straightforward and provides a good starting point for research. Many students, on entering the profession, may be misled into believing this textbook outlives its usefulness; however, it is widely used in law firms as a quick reference book.

D. M. Walker, *The Scottish Legal System*, 6th ed., W. Green, 1992 is a detailed textbook on the history and procedure of Scots law, providing a good account of the development of Scots law and the structure and workings of our present day legal system. The chapter on the repositories of Scots law attempts to detail the main Scottish legal textbooks by subject. Other books of note are: Enid Marshall's *General Principles of Scots Law*, 5th ed., W. Green, 1991; T. B. Smith, *A Short Commentary on the Laws of Scotland*, W. Green, 1962; and *Bell's Dictionary and Digest of the Laws of Scotland*, 7th ed., Bell and Bradfute, 1890.

The most comprehensive contemporary textbook of Scottish private law is D. M. Walker's *Principles of Scottish Private Law*, 4th ed., Oxford University Press, 1987. It is a mini encyclopaedia of Scots law. There is no comprehensive index and the work is divided into four volumes. Volume 1 contains an introduction, international private law and the liability of persons. Volume 2 contains the law of obligations, Volume 3 the law of property and Volume 4 trusts, succession, diligence and others.

All of the main legal textbooks will provide references to more specialised textbooks for research on a particular topic. The last 20 years have seen a considerable expansion in legal publishing in Scotland and this looks set to continue. Whereas formerly the available Scottish textbooks were of a more general nature, this increase in publication has led to the availability of works on specialist subjects.

W. Green now publish books at different levels. The Scottish Universities Law Institute (SULI) series of textbooks, such as Halliday's *Conveyancing Law and Practice* and MacPhail's *Sheriff Court Practice* are the definitive works on their subjects. This level of book is complemented by books pitched at an introductory level and by the publication of casebooks. The subject of delict, for example, is covered by: the definitive work, D. M. Walker, *Delict*, 2nd ed., 1981; Stewart, *An Introduction to the Scots Law of Delict*, 1989; and Stewart, *Casebook on Delict*, 1991, all published by W. Green.

Butterworths publish a series of books in conjunction with the Law Society of Scotland which, although not regarded as definitive works, are nonetheless useful subject guides for practitioners and students alike. Examples are: Cusine, *Standard Securities*, Butterworths, 1991; Gretton, *The Law of Inhibitions and Adjudications*,

Butterworths, 1987; and Scott Robinson, *The Law of Interdict*, Butterworths, 1987.

Naturally, Scots law is as influenced by the will of the European Community as any other European jurisdiction. Modern Scottish textbooks will incorporate references to EEC law, but it is important to remember that older works may not. The subjects in which EEC law is playing an increasingly important part are those in which the laws of the United Kingdom are becoming increasingly harmonised, namely, company, taxation and employment. There are few specifically Scottish works on these topics with the definitive works—such as Palmer's *Company Law*, W. Green/Sweet & Maxwell, and Harvey's *Industrial and Employment Law*, Butterworths (both looseleaf format)—covering the laws of England and Wales, Scotland and the European Community.

# Chapter 4
# Law Reports

## Case Series

As in the rest of the United Kingdom only a few of the cases heard in the Scottish courts will actually be reported, the selection criteria being that they consider a significant point of law. Unreported cases can and are cited but can be difficult to obtain. This chapter deals solely with Scottish reports although the Scottish lawyer will have cause to consult English and EEC decisions.[1]

The main series of Scottish case reports are as follows:

Older reports

The main collections of older reports were reprinted at the beginning of this century by W. Green in their *Scots Revised Reports* series.

*Morison's Dictionary*

The most comprehensive digest of the older cases is contained in *Morison's Dictionary of Decisions* which covers cases in the period 1540 to 1808. The decisions are arranged alphabetically by subject and are numbered sequentially. *Morison's Synopsis* extends the coverage to the period 1808 to 1816. *Brown's Supplement* (cited as B.S.) added further cases to the collection covering the period 1622 to 1794. An index was produced in 1823, *Tait's Index*, which covers *Morison's Dictionary*, *Brown's Supplement* and several of the older collections. *Morison's Dictionary* was reprinted in the *Scots Revised Reports* series, W. Green, and the *Index* provides references to both the chronological decision number and the page on which the decision appears. Decisions will be cited as, for example: (1540) Mor. 5932 or (1540) M. 5932.

---

[1] For these refer to Dane & Thomas, *How To Use A Law Library*, 2nd ed., Sweet & Maxwell, 1987.

*Practicks and private reports*

Until the 18th century there were no full reports of cases; only short notes taken by private individuals who published them as the Practicks. The published Practicks, in chronological order are:

(1) Spotiswoode's *Practicks*, covering 1541 to 1637 (cited as Spot. Prac.);

(2) Hope's *Minor Practicks*, not strictly speaking a Practick in that it does not contain references to decisions but more a summary of Scots law arranged by subject;

(3) Balfour's *Practicks* covering 1469 to 1579 (cited Balf. Prac.); and

(4) Hope's *Major Practicks* covering 1608 to 1633 (cited Hope, Maj. Prac.) and containing decisions arranged by subject.

There are various collections of private reports which cover the period 1621 to 1795. Examples are: Stair's *Decisions*, covering 1661 to 1681 (cited Stair); Fountainhall's *Decisions* covering 1678 to 1712 (cited Fount.); and Kames' *Remarkable Decisions in the Court of Session*, 1716 to 1728 and 1730 to 1752 (cited Kames Rem. Dec.).

*Justiciary (criminal cases)*

Separate private collections of criminal cases were published covering the period 1819 to 1916. Examples are: Shaw 1819 to 1831 (cited Shaw); and Arkley 1846 to 1848 (cited Arkley).

There are several collections of criminal cases covering the period prior to 1819. These include Pitcairn's *Criminal Trials*, covering 1488 to 1624 and McLaurin's (Lord Dreghorn) *Arguments and Decisions in Remarkable Cases before the High Court of Justiciary* covering 1670 to 1773. There are no specific private reports covering the period 1774 to 1818; however, any cases of note are likely to be included in *Morison's Dictionary of Decisions* which covers this period. The *Justiciary Cases* are included in the bound annual volumes of *Session Cases* from 1874 onwards and are paginated separately, for example, 1932 J.C. 18.

*Scottish decisions in the House of Lords*

These are reported in a series of private reports covering the period 1707 to 1865, for example, Shaw 1821 to 1826 (cited Sh. App.) and Bell 1842 to 1850 (cited Bell). The House of Lords private reports were reprinted as part of the *Scots Revised Reports* series, W. Green. In 1865 Kinnear's *Scottish Appeal Cases* was published by Bell & Bradfute, covering the years 1709 to 1864 and arranged by subject. The Scottish appeals to the House of Lords are also reported in the English law reports, such as the *All England Reports* and *Law Reports* (Appeal Cases).

Scottish decisions in the House of Lords are reported in the

*Session Cases* from 1850, but are separately paginated. They are cited, for example, *Harrison* v. *Anderston Foundry Company* (1876) 8 R. (H.L.) 55, in other words, page 55 of volume 8 of the cases reported by Rettie.

*Faculty Collection*
These reports are in three series. The old series covers 1752 to 1808, the new series 1808 to 1825 and the octavo series 1825 to 1841. These are the decisions reported by the reporter of decisions of the Faculty of Advocates. The old and new series are cited by date of decision and F.C.: for example, 25th Feb, 1808; and the octavo series is cited by the volume number and page: for example, 5 Fac. Dec. 88. The *Faculty Collection* was reprinted as part of the *Scots Revised Reports* series, W. Green, in 1905 to 1906.

*Faculty Digest*
This is a digest of cases from 1868 to 1922 which arranges cases by subject with an alphabetical index and includes cases judicially considered. It has been updated by five volumes bringing us up to 1970.

*Scots Digest*
This contains Scottish House of Lords cases from 1707 to 1947 and cases from the superior courts from 1800 to 1947. Cases are arranged by subject.

*Digest*
This is predominantly an English reference source: however, digests of Scottish cases are included.

*Others*
There are other collections of older reports such as *Scottish Shipping cases 1865 to 1890*, W. Green, 1891; and Ross, *Leading cases in the Laws of Scotland*, 1707 to 1849, Sutherland and Knox, 1849. Two other older series of law reports are: *The Scottish Law Reporter* (S.L.R.) which covered cases decided in the Court of Session, High Court of Justiciary, Court of Teinds and House of Lords for the period 1865 to 1924; and *The Scottish Jurist* covering decisions of the same courts in the period 1829 to 1873 (S.J.).

*Sheriff Court Reports*
The *Scottish Law Review* published between 1885 and 1963 by W. Hodge & Co, included reports of the sheriff court. It is cited S.L.R. or S.L. Rev. W. Hodge also published between 1906 and 1936 a collection of sheriff court decisions in the *Sheriff Court Digest* covering the period 1885 to 1944.

Modern Reports

*Session Cases*
These were originally purely the reports of decisions of the Court of Session. Between 1821 and 1906 five series appeared which are cited by the volume number and the initial letter of the five respective editors. The editors are Shaw (1821 to 1838), Dunlop (1838 to 1862), MacPherson (1862 to 1873), Rettie (1873 to 1898), and Fraser (1898 to 1906). Cases from this period are cited by their volume number and the initial letter of the editor's name. For example, a case in volume three of the Rettie series at page 386 would be cited 3 R. 386. The year is occasionally mentioned in round brackets as it is possible to locate the case without knowledge of its year. From 1907 the *Session Cases* are simply cited as S.C. and the year will be given. The *Session Cases* contain three separately numbered collections of reports within each volume. House of Lords cases are cited, for example, 1964 S.C. (H.L.) 52 and included from 1850; Court of Justiciary cases, for example, 1956 J.C. 59 and included from 1874; the Court of Session cases, which form the largest part of each volume, are cited, 1964 S.C. 69. In recent years there have been problems in the production of this series and reporting has lagged somewhat behind that of the *Scots Law Times*.

*Scots Law Times*
Published weekly from 1893 by W. Green it includes articles of legal interest, professional news, Acts of Sederunt and reports including cases from the Court of Session, High Court of Justiciary and the House of Lords. Each series of cases is separately paginated. These are:

(1) Court of Session, High Court of Justiciary and House of Lords reports;
(2) Sheriff court reports;
(3) Scottish Land Court and Lands Tribunal for Scotland reports; and
(4) Notes of recent decisions (before 1982).

Be careful to check the correct section of the book for the case you require. Cases will be cited, for example, S.L.T. (Sh.Ct.) denoting a case in the sheriff court reports section.

*Scottish Criminal Case Reports (published from 1981)*
These are produced by the Law Society of Scotland and contain a commentary on each case. Cases are included from both the Court of Justiciary and the sheriff court. Cases are cited S.C.C.R.

*Scottish Civil Law Reports (from 1987)*
Again these are produced by the Law Society of Scotland and
contain commentary on each case. Cases are included from both the
Court of Session and the sheriff court. Cases are cited S.C.L.R.

*Green's Weekly Digest (from 1986)*
A summary arranged by subject of all cases and decisions brought to
the attention of the publisher, W. Green. The purpose of the service
is to report cases as quickly as possible and important decisions are
for this reason normally reported more fully at a later date in W.
Green's sister publication, the *Scots Law Times*. Cases which
appear in G.W.D. will be digested in *Current Law*, but will not
appear in the case index or *Year Book*.

*Lexis*
A detailed explanation of *Lexis* is given in chapter 2. The Scots
library on *Lexis* contains reported cases from the S.L.T. and S.C.
from 1950 and the complete series of S.C.C.R. and S.C.L.R. Unreported decisions from the Inner House (post 1982) and the Outer
House (post 1985) are available.

All of the reports may not be available in every library. Academic
libraries may have a more extensive collection than those detailed
above. Ask the library staff if any help is needed either to establish if
the book is held or to use the book itself. For a more extensive list of
all Scottish reports see D. M. Walker's *The Scottish Legal System*,
W. Green, 1992.

**How to Find Cases**

Remember that any cases found will contain references to cases on
similar points of law and may also be checked for any subsequent
cases in which they were judicially considered.

Citations

When checking a citation many law libraries will hold a copy of
Raistrick's book entitled *The Index to Legal Citations and Abbreviations*, Professional Books, 1981. If your library does not hold this
book alternative sources are the tables at the front of any general
textbook, the tables at the front of *Current Law* or each volume of
the *Stair Memorial Encyclopaedia* or *Halsbury's Laws of England*.

Finding cases by name only

The most frequent problem in locating a case is having an incom-
plete reference, where the name of the case is known but the
citation is not. There are various sources which can be used.

*Current Law Case Citator*
A detailed explanation of the *Current Law Case Citator* is given in chapter 2. The Scottish index to cases is at the back of the *Case Citator* in the bound volumes, in the monthly parts the Scottish cases are simply listed in the main index. Cases are arranged alphabetically with their citation and a reference to the relevant summary in the appropriate *Current Law Year Book*. The citators also list cases judicially considered.

*Books*
Check the table of cases in a book on the appropriate subject.

*Law Reports*
Check the indexes to *Scots Law Times*, cumulative index to *Green's Weekly Digest*, 1986 to 1991, *All England Reports*, *Times Law Reports*, etc.

*Legal Journals Index*
A detailed explanation of the *Legal Journals Index* is given in chapter 2. Check in the case index for 1986 onwards. Where a reference is made to the case in a particular journal article, refer to the article itself which will provide a citation for the case. Cases are cited by either party which can be very useful where only the defender's name is known.

*Daily Law Reports Index*
A detailed explanation of the *Daily Law Reports Index* is given in chapter 2. Check under the parties' names.

*Lexis*
A detailed explanation of *Lexis* is given in chapter 2. Searching under the parties' names may find both a reference and copy of the report.

*The Law Reports Index*
This is an index to the main English law reports, namely the *Law Reports* covering appeal, chancery, etc., *Weekly Law Reports* and *Industrial Cases Reports*. This table also refers to reports from other series such as the *Road Traffic Reports*. Important Scottish cases will also be noted.

Older cases

When checking citations for older cases check the textbooks again. Cases referred to frequently will often be quoted in textbooks on the appropriate topic.
Alternatively you may wish to consult one of the older indexes as follows.

*Faculty Digest*
If the case is not listed in the table of those digested within the text, it may be listed within the pages of the cases judicially referred to. The *Faculty Digest* covers cases from the period 1868 to 1970.

*The Index to Morison's Dictionary*
This index covers the period 1540 to 1820 and provides a reference to the case reports in either the *Dictionary* itself, *Brown's Supplement* or other old collections.

*The Digest*
Checking through the consolidated tables of cases provides a reference to a volume number. The case table in the appropriate volume in turn refers to the appropriate entry. As the digest is predominantly an English reference work Scottish cases are referred to after their English counterparts with citations given at the end of each entry.

Finding cases by subject

A good starting point is either the *Stair Memorial Encyclopaedia* or *Halsbury's Laws of England* where appropriate. A general reference book such as D. M. Walker's *Principles of Scottish Private Law* or Gloag & Henderson's *Introduction to the Law of Scotland*, both published by W. Green, may be of use. There are increasingly few areas of Scots law which do not have a dedicated text book and an appropriate work should be consulted wherever possible. Other sources include the following.

*Current Law*
A detailed explanation of *Current Law* is given in chapter 2. Check the relevant Scottish subject heading in both the year books and monthly parts.

*Legal Journals Index*
A detailed explanation of the *Legal Journals Index* is given in chapter 2. Check the subject headings and mention of any appropriate cases. The *Scots Law Times* is indexed in this publication and therefore all cases are indexed by subject.

*Law Report Indexes*
Check the subject index to *Scots Law Times* which is contained in each volume and issued cumulatively in each weekly part, the 1986 to 1991 cumulative index to *Green's Weekly Digest* and its regular cumulative updates. Case series such as the *Industrial Relations Law Reports* or the *All England Reports* also provide their own detailed subject indexes and this may be a very efficient way of locating cases. The *Industrial Relations Law Reports*, for example, are the main series of case reports for employment cases and, if this

is your field of interest, checking the detailed index may eliminate unnecessary searching. The *Times Law Reports* index or *Daily Law Reports* index may be used for very recent cases.

### Lexis

A detailed explanation of *Lexis* is given in chapter 2. The primary benefit of the *Lexis* database is that cases are included in full text and are retrievable by any word or combination of words therein. Cases can be located by searching under any subject key word which you consider relevant. The system retrieves literally and the search strategy, therefore, should be considered carefully before accessing *Lexis* as time online is costly.

## Finding cases on legislation

### Current Law Legislation Citator

A detailed explanation of the *Current Law Legislation Citator* is given in chapter 2. Check under the appropriate piece of legislation and any cases on an Act or particular section of an Act will be given. Check the legislation citators in both the bound volumes and monthly parts.

### The Legal Journals Index

A detailed explanation of the *Legal Journals Index* is given in chapter 2. Check the legislation citator which will refer to articles discussing a particular aspect of legislation. The articles themselves may contain reference to specific cases which may also be of interest.

### Law Reports Indexes

The *Daily Law Reports* index and *Times Law Reports* index both contain an index to the cases by legislation considered. Similarly in the alphabetical subject index to the *Scots Law Times* under the words 'statutes and orders' legislation judicially considered is listed in an alphabetical format.

### Textbooks

Textbooks provide an index of legislation mentioned throughout the work. The index will provide references to the appropriate sections in the work where the legislation is considered and relevant case law on the subject may also be found.

### Lexis

A detailed explanation of *Lexis* is given in chapter 2. As previously explained, *Lexis* is a full text retrieval system. It is therefore competent to search by the name and section of a piece of legislation. The search will retrieve cases which discuss or mention the legislation required.

Current status of a case

It is very important to check the status of a case as it may have been reversed by a subsequent decision or considered in other cases.

*Current Law Case Citator*
A detailed explanation of the *Current Law Case Citator* is given in chapter 2. The *Citator* lists cases from 1947, however, the table of cases judicially considered will obviously cover a much wider time span. The *Case Citator* will state whether a case has been approved, disapproved, reversed, distinguished, etc., and will refer you to the *Current Law* paragraph number where the case decision is digested. Remember always to check both the Scottish and English case tables. The Scottish case table appears at the rear of the tables.

*The Faculty Digest*
This is primarily of use for older cases. Check in the table of cases judicially considered and update in the subsequent volumes.

*Lexis*
A detailed explanation of *Lexis* is given in chapter 2. It is possible to simply search under the name of a case on *Lexis* and this will provide a list of cases in which the name appears, in other words, the original case and any subsequent appeal or case in which it is judicially considered.

*Law Reports Index*
Check the tables of cases judicially considered.

# Chapter 5

# Legislation and Government Publications

## Bills

Public Bills are those relating to matters of public policy. Private Bills are those for the particular interest or benefit of any person or body. When they have passed through all their parliamentary stages and received Royal Assent they then become Acts of Parliament or statutes and are published by Her Majesty's Stationery Office (HMSO).

Finding information about a Bill

Use the Progress of Bills section which is situated at the rear of the *Current Law* monthly parts to establish what stage a Bill has reached. Alternatively use the *House of Commons Weekly Information Bulletin*, published by HMSO, which may be available in your library, and consult the Progress of Bills tables. More detail on the progress of all Bills, both private and public, is given in this publication. The *Bulletin* will state where a Bill has been published and will provide a source for obtaining copies of any private Bills required. Public Bills are cited with the initials of the House from which the proposing MP belongs. They are also given a chronological number. If the number of the Bill is given in square brackets the Bill is presently in the House of Commons, if the number is enclosed in round brackets it is presently being considered in the House of Lords. For example, H.L. 1991–92 Offshore Safety Bill [43], denotes that the Bill was introduced in the House of Lords, in the parliamentary session 1991–92 and that the Bill is presently under consideration in the House of Commons.

**Statutes**

Early statutes

Scots Acts prior to 1707 are in the *Acts of the Parliament of Scotland 1124–1707* edited by Thomson and Innes and known as the Record Edition. Statutes still in force in 1964 were reprinted by HMSO in the *Acts of the Parliament of Scotland 1424–1707*, which was published in 1966.

Modern statutes

There are various published editions of the statutes now available. *The Statutes Revised*, 3rd ed. 1235 to 1948 prints in chronological order statutes still in force in 1948. (It does not include pre-1707 Scottish Acts.)

   *The Statutes Revised* is continued up-to-date by *The Public General Statutes*. HMSO publishes copies of new Acts on their Royal Assent and these are bound together and published at the year end. The *Scots Statutes Revised* 1707 to 1900 includes Acts only applicable to Scotland (Scots statutes). It continues as *Scots Statutes* from 1901 to 1948 and from 1949 becomes *Scottish Current Law Statutes*. From 1991 onwards the service has been incorporated into the *Current Law Statutes*. The Acts are published with commentary. The *Current Law* service produces the text of the Act initially without commentary (printed on blue paper) and several weeks later the Act will be reprinted on white paper with commentary. Bound volumes are published at the year end.

Law Report Statutes

These are produced in a similar format to the Public General Acts.

Indexes for all the above statutes are both alphabetical and chronological.

Statutes in Force

This is an HMSO publication which began in 1972. Each Act in force is printed as a separate pamphlet. The looseleaf volumes are arranged by subject with all Acts on the one subject being gathered together in the one volume. A noter up, listing subsequent amendments to the Acts enclosed, is available at the front of each volume and when an Act is substantially changed it will be reprinted incorporating amendments.

Others

The other statutes series include *Halsbury's Statutes* and Butterworths *Selected Statutes* which totally exclude those Acts only applicable to Scotland

Lexis

A detailed explanation of *Lexis* is given in chapter 2. *Lexis* is of limited use for Scottish legislation. All legislation exclusive to Scotland is excluded from the database. In the past any references of UK Acts applicable solely to Scotland were actually removed from the text of a statute. This situation has now been remedied and Scottish provisions contained in UK Acts from January 1980 appear and amendments are incorporated. *Lexis* has no imminent plans for including purely Scottish legislation.

**How to find an Act**

Where the year and the name of the Act is given check the indexes to any of the above series of statutes to establish the chapter number of the Act, namely, the chronological number given to statutes throughout the year. If the name of the Act only is given, check the alphabetical index at the front of the *Current Law Legislation Citator*, or the *Index to the Statutes* by the appropriate subject to establish the year and chapter number. Statutes are normally stored in chapter order.

  Older Acts are cited by year and chapter number or if a reference is made to the record edition the citation will be to the volume and page number. Where the older regnal years are given, to convert this to the calendar year check the *Parliament House Book* or ask the librarian. Pre-1963 statutes will be given in the regnal year form, for example, Education (Scotland) Act 9 & 10 George VI, Chapter 72, in other words, the 72nd Act passed in the parliamentary session which extended over the 9th and 10th years of the reign of George VI.

How to find an Act by subject

*Index to the Statutes*
A detailed explanation of the *Index to the Statutes* is given in chapter 2. This provides an alphabetical subject index to the statutes with a separate section for Scottish legislation at the end of each subject. Check the subject area in which you are interested and note down any Acts listed. The *Index* is quite specific and provides references to individual sections of some Acts.

*Current Law Year Books*
A detailed explanation of the *Current Law Year Books* is given in

chapter 2. These list statutes published in any year under the appropriate subject heading. This can be followed through in the monthly parts.

*Textbooks*
Check a major textbook to establish the main statutes on the subject. The *Stair Memorial Encyclopaedia* is ideal for this as it is constantly updated.

## Checking if an Act is in force

*The Act itself*
The date of commencement is normally given at the end of the Act either by stating a specific time period after which the Act shall come into force or by specifying that the Act will come into force as directed in a commencement order by the minister concerned. The latter method is the more common, particularly for large statutes and several commencement orders may be made under the one Act.

*Is it in Force?*
This is an annual Butterworths publication covering the Acts of England, Wales and Scotland from 1966 onwards. The format of the book is such that the Acts are listed alphabetically within each year and the years are dealt with in chronological order. Look up the year and chapter number of the Act required and details will be given as to what sections of the Act are in force and what the enacting legislation was.

*Current Law Legislation Citator*
A more detailed explanation of *Current Law* is given in chapter 2. The *Legislation Citators* are arranged chronologically: turn to the appropriate year and check the chapter number of the statute that you are interested in. Checking under the commencement section of the Act will show whether any commencement orders have been made. Update this in the citator section of the *Monthly Digest*. Where the Act has received Royal Assent in the current year check the alphabetical table at the back of the most recent *Current Law Monthly Digest* to establish what sections, if any, are in force.

*Index to Government Orders*
A detailed explanation of the *Index to Government Orders* is given in chapter 2. Check the table of statutes at the front to establish in which section a Statutory Instrument would be covered. Turn to that section and check if any commencement orders have been made. Update with *Current Law*.

*Journals*
Journals such as the *Solicitors' Journal* will provide a list of new commencement orders. The *Journal of the Law Society of Scotland*

and the *Scots Law Times* also provide updates on which Acts have recently come into force. However, these are of more use as a general updating service than as a definitive guide to which sections of an Act are in force. Several of the English journals will also be of use, for example, the *New Law Journal* and the *Law Society Gazette*.

### HMSO Daily, Weekly or Monthly Lists

A detailed explanation of the HMSO lists is given in chapter 2. If a commencement order is due for publication check in recent issues of the *Daily List* or *Weekly List*.

### Lexis

A detailed explanation of *Lexis* is given in chapter 2. Each section of the statutes contains a date in force section. This is subject to the limitations of using *Lexis* when researching Scottish legislation.

Checking the current status of a statute

### Current Law Legislation Citator

A detailed explanation of the *Current Law Legislation Citator* is given in chapter 2. Look up the year and chapter number. Information is given on any amendments and appeals to the Act and any cases under particular sections. The amendments will be found alongside the sections to which they pertain. The amendments refer only to years, chapters and sections; check the *Citator* itself or the chronological table of statutes to establish the statute title.

### Chronological Table of the Statutes

A detailed explanation of the *Chronological Table of the Statutes* is given in chapter 2. Go to the year in question and check the chapter number to establish the statute title. Where the title of the Act appears in italics it has been repealed. Where it appears in bold type then it is still, at least in part, in force. Amendments will be given with references.

### Local Acts

These are indexed in the *Chronological Table of the Statutes* in Section 4. A fuller list of all personal Acts is available from the Law Commission for England and Wales. There is also an HMSO classified subject index entitled *The Index to Local and Personal Acts 1801 to 1947* and a *Supplementary Index to Local and Personal Acts 1948 to 1966* which is continued by an annual table and index. All private Acts are printed by HMSO, however, they are not published in bound volumes. An annual list of private Acts is published by HMSO and the Acts are classified into ordinary private Acts, public Acts of a local character, including Provisional

Orders and Order Confirmation Acts and personal Acts (very few of these are now presented). Remember that Acts which sound local may not always be so: for example, the Greenwich Hospital Act 1990 is in fact a public Act.

Finding local Acts

The chapter number of local Acts is given in small roman numerals. Larger libraries such as the Advocates Library will have a full collection of local and personal Acts.

## Statutory Instruments

A Statutory Instrument may be entitled Order, Regulation, Rule, Act of Sederunt or Act of Adjournal. A date of commencement is always stipulated. Citation of Statutory Instruments will be either by year and number, for example, 1990/443 or by title and year, for example, Milk Quota (Calculation of Standard Quota) (Scotland) Amendment Order 1990. Statutory Instruments which are applicable solely to Scotland are also given a separate Scottish chronological number. Those which are commencement orders, in other words, bringing a part or the whole of an Act into force, are also given an additional chronological number. For example, The Law Reform (Miscellaneous Provisions) (Scotland) Act 1990 (Commencement No. 7) Order 1991 is cited as 1991/1903 (C. 53) (S.157).

Acts of Sederunt are the subordinate legislation of the Court of Session. Acts of Adjournal are the subordinate legislation of the High Court of Justiciary to regulate criminal procedure. These are published by HMSO as Statutory Instruments and are also available in full in the appropriate year in the *Scots Law Times*. They are reproduced in bound volumes of the *Scottish Current Law Statutes* for the years to 1991 only. All Acts of Sederunt and Adjournal currently in force will be found in the *Parliament House Book* published by W. Green.

Finding the full text of a Statutory Instrument

*HMSO*
All Statutory Instruments are published by HMSO and annual bound volumes are available. These are also now being produced in CD ROM format and several back years are available. The bound volumes of the paper copies are normally several years behind in production. The annual bound volumes are issued in three parts. Pre-1961 volumes contain a numerical list of Statutory Instruments in the first part and the Statutory Instruments themselves are arranged by subject. From 1961 the Statutory Instruments are

arranged chronologically with a cumulative subject-index in each part. The final part contains a subject-list of local Statutory Instruments and a full numerical list.

*Looseleaf encyclopaedias*
These often contain the full text of any Statutory Instruments relevant to the subject. The *Parliament House Book* contains the full text of all Acts of Sederunt and Statutory Instruments pertaining to the work of the courts, for example, regarding legal aid. Other examples are *Renton & Brown's Criminal Procedure* and *Armour on Valuation for Rating*, both published by W. Green.

*Halsbury's Statutory Instruments*
Published by Butterworths this is primarily an English work and does not cover purely Scottish Statutory Instruments, however, it may be useful for the full text of the United Kingdom Statutory Instruments. The work consists of bound volumes in which the Statutory Instruments are arranged by subject and two looseleaf volumes which update these and contain the full text of any major Statutory Instruments.

*Current Law*
A detailed explanation of *Current Law* is given in chapter 2. Summaries of all Statutory Instruments are given in the *Monthly Digests* and *Year Books*. Where only brief information is required, for example a commencement date, this may be sufficient. *Current Law* at present provides both an alphabetical subject index and chronological index to Statutory Instruments in the *Year Books*. The *Monthly Digests* contain only an alphabetical listing.

Finding Statutory Instruments on a subject

*Index to Government Orders*
A detailed explanation of the *Index to Government Orders* is given in chapter 2. Statutory Instruments are listed under the appropriate subject headings. This covers all orders in force on the date of publication of the book. Check under the appropriate heading required.

*Textbooks*
Check the relevant subject volume of *Halsbury's Statutory Instruments*. Check a text book or relevant looseleaf encyclopaedia. The *Stair Memorial Encyclopaedia* will mention any relevant Statutory Instruments by subject.

**Official lists**
HMSO publish a monthly list of Statutory Instruments with an

annual cumulation. This contains a main-subject sequence and cumulative alphabetical and numerical indexes. This can be supplemented by the Daily List.

Checking the current status of a Statutory Instrument

*Table of Government Orders*
A detailed explanation of the *Table of Government Orders* is given in chapter 2. Similar to the *Chronological Table of the Statutes* this lists Statutory Instruments in chronological order and details any amendments.

*Current Law*
A detailed explanation of *Current Law* is given in chapter 2. Tables of Statutory Instruments are at the end of the *Legislation Citator* and show amendments for Statutory Instruments affected in the period which the citator covers. This is not, unfortunately, updated in the *Monthly Digests*. Note that in the citator covering the period 1947–1971 a reference to 68/300 would refer to paragraph 300 of the 1968 yearbook, whereas in later citators a reference to 85/88 would refer to S.I. 85 of 1988. Tables of Statutory Instruments affected during the year appear in each *Current Law Year Book*. This lists Statutory Instruments affected during the year in chronological order with amendments and repeals made.

Locating a Statutory Instrument by enacting legislation

*Index to Government Orders*
A detailed explanation of the *Index to Government Orders* is given in chapter 2. Check under the list of statutes at the beginning of volume one to establish the subject heading under which any Statutory Instruments would be mentioned. Refer to the subject section and any Statutory Instruments made will be listed under the appropriate statute.

*Current Law Legislation Citator*
A detailed explanation of the *Current Law Legislation Citator* is given in chapter 2. Turn to the year and chapter number of the statute required and check under the particular section of the Act to establish whether any Statutory Instruments have been made.

Details of commencement orders for particular Acts will be found in both the Dates of Commencement tables in *Current Law* and in *Is It In Force?*

# Chapter 6
# Journals

Journal articles are important for two reasons: they may act as a vehicle for updating your knowledge in a particular field and they may provide the only information on a relatively obscure area of the law. Journals normally fall into five different categories, namely: weekly publications, which aim to provide an updating service; academic journals, published usually quarterly; professional journals, such as the *Journal of the Law Society of Scotland*; specialist journals such as *Public Procurement Law*; and foreign periodicals which may be useful for comparative law.

It is important to research journals as comprehensively as possible. The following legal journals are those published in Scotland, however, many aspects of Scottish law are becoming increasingly harmonised, such as employment and company law, and accordingly it is also necessary to check the UK journals.

Scotland does not have an extensive collection of independent journals. Arguably the two most important are:

(1) *Journal of the Law Society of Scotland*: published monthly from 1956 onwards. This is the solicitors' profession's journal and as such contains articles on specific areas of Scots law, professional news, occasional legal updates, book reviews and brief law reports.

(2) *Scots Law Times*: published weekly by W. Green from 1893. In addition to law reports and articles it contains professional information and the full text of Acts of Sederunt.

The other Scottish legal journals are:

(1) *Juridical Review*: published biannually by W. Green, 1889 to 1991 and three times per year from 1992 onwards. This is

a refereed academic journal and contains articles and book reviews.

(2) *SCOLAG*: published monthly by the Scottish Legal Action Group, 1975 onwards. Contains case reports on selected fields of law such as housing and welfare law.

(3) *Scottish Law Gazette*: published quarterly by the Council of the Scottish Law Agents Society from 1932 onwards. Contains a wide spread of articles and news.

(4) *Scottish Planning Law and Practice*: published three times per annum by the Planning Exchange and the Law Society of Scotland. Contains articles and case reports on planning.

(5) *Impecunias*: published quarterly from 1991 by the Institute of Chartered Accountants in Scotland and the Law Society of Scotland. This is a specialist insolvency journal.

**How to Find Journal Articles**

There are several commercial publications now available. However, remember that all journals will have an index and if checking for an article in a particular journal check the index first.

The main indexing sources are as follows.

Legal Journals Index

A detailed explanation of the *Legal Journals Index* is given in chapter 2. For articles after 1986 check in the appropriate index. Articles are indexed alphabetically by subject, author, case discussed or legislation discussed. It is thus possible to locate articles on a specific subject, by a specific author, by checking under the name of any case which may be discussed or any legislation which may be discussed. A list of journal abbreviations used will be found at the beginning of the index.

Current Law

A detailed explanation of *Current Law* is given in chapter 2. There is an alphabetical index to articles published throughout the year in each of the *Current Law Year Books*. The articles index will be found, in those volumes prior to 1991, at the end of the English materials and before the Scottish. From 1991 onwards the index is at the back of the volume. Check under the appropriate subject heading. Check that the particular section includes Scottish materials as in some of the older volumes Scottish articles may actually be listed alphabetically by subject under the heading Scotland. For recent articles check the appropriate subject heading within the Scottish part of the *Current Law Monthly Digests*. Articles are listed at the end of the appropriate subject section. A list of journal abbreviations used will be found at the beginning of *Current Law*.

Index to Legal Periodicals

Published monthly in the United States from 1908 onwards, this covers journals from the United Kingdom, Canada, Ireland, Australia and New Zealand. Use the index by searching either under the subject or author of the article, the entries being provided in one single alphabetical sequence. Separate indexes cover cases, legislation and book reviews. This index is available on CD ROM and online.

Index to Foreign Legal Periodicals

Published quarterly from 1960 onwards, this indexes articles on international and comparative law. It is important to remember, however, that many of the articles will not be in English. A directory of periodicals, such as Ulrichs, will establish in what language a journal is published.

Lexis

A detailed explanation of this source is given in chapter 2. *Lexis* contains a UK journals library and coverage extends to the *Journal of the Law Society of Scotland* 1990 onwards, *Estates Gazette* 1991 onwards, *The Law Society Gazette* 1986 onwards and the *New Law Journal* from 1986 onwards.

Textbooks will often list relevant journal articles for further reading; for example, McDonald's *Conveyancing Manual*, Park Place Publishing, 1989. However, this source is unlikely to be of use for very current articles. The annual abridgements to *Halsbury's Laws of England* provide a list of relevant articles published during the year at the beginning of the appropriate subject heading.

**Obtaining Copies of Articles Found**

On locating an item, check the list of abbreviations which will appear at the front of the index used to establish the journal title. Check your library's journal holdings list to establish if the article is immediately available. If not ask your librarian to obtain a copy or refer you to another library. Legal Information Resources Limited, the publishers of the *Legal Journals Index*, will, for a fee, provide copies of the majority of the items which they index.

Newspaper articles

If checking for newspaper articles, various newspapers produce indexes, such as, *The Times Index*, *The Financial Times Index*. These are likely to be available only in larger libraries. Other publications such as *Keesing's Record of World Events* may help to establish the date of a specific event which may narrow down the time period to be covered. Many of the larger libraries will have holdings of the main newspapers and the larger papers will have their own libraries which may accept telephone enquiries. There are several electronic databases commercially available which provide a full text retrieval service for the main UK newspapers, such as *Textline* and *Profile*. For information on these databases contact your local Business Information Service: in Glasgow this will be in the Mitchell Library, telephone 041 248 3997; and in Edinburgh at the Science Building of the National Library for Scotland, telephone 031 667 9554.

# Chapter 7

# European Community Law

Scotland as part of the United Kingdom is as bound by the laws of the EEC as any other Member State. Membership began in 1973 but, with the deadline for a Single European Market now upon us, awareness of the EEC has become more prevalent within the Scottish legal profession. Few Scottish libraries will have a comprehensive collection of EEC materials, however, EEC law is an important part of Scots law and it is a necessary requirement of the competent lawyer to be aware of what resources there are and how best to exploit them. EEC law can no longer be viewed as a separate area of law such as environmental law but must be accepted as influencing all areas of Scots law.

The primary legislation of the EEC is outlined in its treaties and amendments, and in its secondary legislation including decisions, regulations, directives and recommendations, which outline the method by which its objectives are to be met. The *Official Journal of the European Communities* (OJ), publishes the latter in two series. The C series covers information and notes, including case decisions. The L series covers legislation, including draft legislation. In the past five years particularly there has been an explosion of books published on EEC law. The nature of EEC law is such that it changes rapidly and because of its breadth and complexity it can be difficult and costly to keep abreast of EEC developments.

**EEC Sources**

Encyclopaedia of European Communities Law

Published by Sweet & Maxwell this is a multi-volume looseleaf work which covers both the founding treaties, subordinate legislation and UK sources. The work is updated and amendments are incorporated into the text of legislation, which is very useful. The work is never current as updates are slow to appear and the index is not ideal. Coverage, however, is wide.

## The Common Market Reporter

Published by Commercial Clearing House (CCH) this is a much smaller work, updated far more frequently but necessarily selective in its coverage. The indexes are extensive and the work provides the full text of the major treaties and some legislation with amendments being incorporated into the body of the text. However, the work suffers from being produced on poor quality paper and is not well served by a dual page numbering system. Cases are reported speedily.

## Other sources

These include Butterworths' *Encyclopaedia of European Community Law*. This developed from the two EEC volumes published as part of *Halsbury's Laws of England* and is a looseleaf updated work. Butterworths also produce various EEC encyclopaedias, for example *Competition Law* and *EEC Company Law*.

## Electronic Sources

EEC information is also available online. *Lexis* contains the EEC official database, *CELEX*, which is an edited version of the *Official Journal*. *Lexis* is accessible but is subject to the constraints of *CELEX*, which was designed originally as an in-house European Commission database and it is not very user friendly. There is also reasonable case coverage which includes all the decisions of the ECR. The European Commission offers other databases as part of its EUROBASES service in addition to *CELEX*, covering, for example, their press releases (*RAPID*) and legislation relating solely to the Single Market (*INFO92*). The Department of Trade and Industry (DTI) offers its own database entitled *Spearhead* which extends solely to Single Market information. Contact *Lexis*, the European Commission or the DTI for more information on their respective databases.[1]

### Finding Legislation

The text of the EEC treaties are reprinted in the *Abridged Version of the Treaties*, a small publication published by the European

---

[1] For further information on European Communities databases, see J. Jeffries' article in the *Law Librarian*, Sweet & Maxwell, December 1989.

Communities Office for Publications and available from HMSO, which is the main UK agency for EEC publications. They are also reprinted in the encyclopaedias mentioned above. HMSO also provide a service entitled SCANFAX whereby they will fax items from the OJ for a fee.

Citations

The citation of EC legislation is an indication of its format. Regulations are given in the form of number then year, such as, 1629/70, and directives or decisions in the form of year then number, such as, 72/182. All legislation is published in the text of the *Official Journal*.

The Directory of Community Legislation in Force and Other Acts of the Community Institutions

This is a two volume work published twice yearly. It appears fairly formidable but is easy to use if a little time is devoted to reading the section entitled 'Information for readers'. The work is in two volumes, Volume 2 providing both a chronological and alphabetical index to all items listed in Volume 1. The alphabetical subject index refers to the page in Volume 1 where legislation on that subject will appear. The chronological index lists materials by year, type of document and serial number of document. For example the Directive 79/1072 appears as 379 L 1072. The number 3 is a reference designed for use with the EEC database *CELEX*, then the year is given, followed by L denoting directive and finally 1072 which denotes that the document is number 1072 of 1979. The index refers the reader to page 556 in Volume 1 where the directive appears as the Eighth Directive on Harmonisation Relating to Turnover Taxes and the OJ reference is given. Modifications and amendments are also given with their appropriate OJ references.

Index to the Official Journal

This is published monthly and cumulated annually. There are two parts. The alphabetical index provides an index alphabetically by subject to all material contained within the OJ for the period indexed. The methodological table divides the materials chronologically into legislation and information and notices and includes information concerning the European Court of Justice.

European Communities Legislation Current Status

To trace legislation on a subject use Butterworths' *European Communities Legislation Current Status*. This is an annual publication which includes a subject index to all EEC legislation post 1973. Subject indexes covering legislation are also included in the encyclopaedias previously mentioned.

Current Law

A detailed explanation of *Current Law* is given in chapter 2. *Current Law* contains a section on EEC law and checking through the relevant sections of the *Current Law Year Books* and *Monthly Digests* will highlight recent legislation.

### Establishing the Current Status of Legislation

Use all of the above sources. In addition, Sweet and Maxwell began publication in January 1992 of the *Monthly Digest of European Law* which covers the laws of all European countries and EEC law. Information is listed by subject.

To establish whether EEC legislation has yet been implemented in the United Kingdom, check the *Encyclopaedia of European Communities Law*. The EC publish an index which details the provisions of the Single Market and the enacting legislation of each Member State. This is available from HMSO, is updated regularly and is also available on *CELEX*. Butterworths *European Communities Legislation Current Status* introduced in 1992, as part of their service, a bound volume detailing UK enacting legislation under the relevant EC legislation.

### Finding Cases

Cases may be cited by their case number, for example, 50/87, or by the name of the parties. The official series of law reports of the EC is the Reports of Cases before the Courts (ECR), published from 1954 onwards. These reports are slow to appear, primarily because of the time taken for translations, and the commercially produced *Common Market Law Reports* or *CCH Reports* are more commonly used. EEC cases are indexed in *Current Law*, and by name and number in the *Common Market Law Reports* and in the *CCH Common Market Reports*. The CCH index also indexes the cases by community legislation considered and lists cases judicially considered.

It is possible to receive copies of the Courts Weekly Listings of Hearings and Weekly Summary of Cases direct from the European Court of Justice. The European Law Centre, run by Sweet &

Maxwell, produces a range of specialist EEC reports, for example, EEC employment cases.

### Current Status of a Case

This will be given in the *Current Law Case Citator* by checking under the parties names. EEC cases are also covered in the *Digest*, although very recent cases are unlikely to be listed. All modern textbooks will include coverage of relevant EEC cases and if tracing a reference it may be worth checking the table of cases on the appropriate subject for a citation. The *Common Market Law Reports* also contain a table of cases judicially considered.

### Current Awareness Sources

It is difficult to keep up-to-date on EEC law and there are many journals which endeavour to make it easier. If available, *Agence Europe* (daily), Sweet & Maxwell's *European Current Law Digest* (monthly) or Butterworths' *EC Brief* (weekly) do provide current information.

The Commission produces many indexes to help with tracing Commission documents and draft legislation and the Commission Office in Edinburgh is a good source of information. The DTI Single Market Hotline may also assist. The main collections of EEC information in Scotland are available at:

### Office of the European Commission
9 Alva Street
Edinburgh
EH2 4PH
Tel: 031 225 2058

European Information Centres:

**EuroInfo Centre**
21 Bothwell Street
Glasgow G2 6NR
Tel: 041 221 0999

**Highland Opportunity Limited**
Development Department
Highland Regional Council
Glenurquhart Road
Inverness IV3 5NX
Tel: 0463 243121

European Documentation Centres:

**Aberdeen EDC**
University of Aberdeen
Queen Mother Library
Meston Walk
Aberdeen
AB9 2UE
Tel: 0224 272587

**Dundee EDC**
University of Dundee
The Law Library
Scrymgeour Building
Park Place
Dundee DD1 4HN
Tel: 0382 23181

**Edinburgh EDC**
Europa Library
University of Edinburgh
Old College
South Bridge
Edinburgh
EH8 9YL
Tel: 031 650 2041

**Glasgow EDC**
Glasgow University Library
Hillhead Street
Glasgow
G12 8QE
Tel. 041 339 8855

# Appendix
## **Summary of Sources**

### Abbreviations

D. Raistrick's *Index to Legal Citations and Abbreviations,* Professional Books, 1981
Table in *Stair Memorial Encyclopaedia of the Laws of Scotland*
*Legal Journals Index*, Legal Information Resources Limited, 1986
*Current Law*, W. Green/Sweet & Maxwell

### Books

Check the library catalogue whether in printed or electronic format. The catalogue is usually available by author, subject and title.

### Bibliographies

D. M. Walker's *The Scottish Legal System*, W. Green/Sweet & Maxwell, 1992. Consult the chapter on the repositories of Scots law which lists the main textbooks by subject.
*Stair Memorial Encyclopaedia.*
Ask the librarian for information on more detailed legal bibliographies.

### Cases

Where parties only are known, consult one of the following:

(1) *Current Law Case Citator*
(2) The *Digest*
(3) Case tables in *Stair*
(4) *Faculty Digest*
(5) *Scots Digest*
(6) Index to *Morison's Dictionary*

For recent cases consult:

(1) Latest *Current Law Monthly Digest*
(2) *Daily Law Reports Index*
(3) Summaries of cases in weekly journals
(4) Index to S.L.T. or *Green's Weekly Digest*

By subject:

(1) Appropriate volume of *Stair* or textbook
(2) The *Scots Digest*
(3) *Current Law Year Books*
(4) *Scots Law Times* or *Green's Weekly Digest*
(5) *Legal Journals Index*
(6) *Lexis*

By legislation considered:

(1) *Current Law Legislation Citator*
(2) *Legal Journals Index*
(3) Law Reports Indexes
(4) Textbooks
(5) *Lexis*

Tracing the subsequent judicial history of a case:

(1) *Current Law Case Citator* and latest *Monthly Digest*
(2) *Faculty Digest* (older cases)
(3) *Lexis*

Journal articles on a case:

(1) *Legal Journals Index*
(2) *Current Law Case Citator* (journal articles are in square brackets)
(3) Indexes to individual periodicals, such as *Journal of the Law Society of Scotland*.

## Directories

The *White Book*, *The Scottish Law Directory*, T. & T. Clark
The *Blue Book*, Butterworths
A law library will contain several foreign legal directories such as Martindale Hubbell and frequently financial directories such as Crawfords.

**General Statements of the Law**

*Stair Memorial Encyclopaedia of the Laws of Scotland*
The institutional writings
Gloag and Henderson's *Introduction to the Law of Scotland*

**Government Publications**

HMSO daily, weekly, monthly, annual and five yearly indexes of
  government publications
HMSO sectional lists of government publications
*Current Law Year Books*
HMSO in print and various indexes to British Official Papers not
  published by HMSO
*Committee Reports* published by HMSO indexed by chairman
The library catalogue

**Journal Articles**

By subject:

  (1) *Legal Journals Index*
  (2) *Current Law*
  (3) Relevant textbooks

By case:

  (1) *Legal Journals Index*
  (2) *Current Law Case Citator*
  (3) Indexes to specialist journals such as *Scottish Planning Law
  and Practice*

By legislation:

  (1) *Legal Journals Index*
  (2) *Current Law Legislation Citator*

To locate journals check the library's journal holdings list or ask the
  librarian

**Statutes**

By subject:

  (1) *Index to the Statutes*
  (2) *Stair Memorial Encyclopaedia of the Laws of Scotland*
  (3) *Current Law Statutes* and *Current Law Year Books*

Is it in force or amended:

(1) *Is It In Force?*
(2) *Chronological Table of the Statutes*
(3) *Current Law Legislation Citator*

Any cases:

(1) *Current Law Legislation Citator*
(2) Indexes in *Stair Memorial Encyclopaedia*
(3) *Faculty Digest*

Any journal articles:

(1) *Current Law Legislation Citator*
(2) *Legal Journals Index*

Any Statutory Instruments under an Act:

(1) *Current Law Legislation Citator*
(2) *Index to Government Orders*

**Statutory Instruments**
Is the Statutory Instrument in force or amended:

(1) *Table of Government Orders*
(2) *Current Law Legislation Citator*

Indexes to Statutory Instruments:

(1) *Index to Government Orders*
(2) *Halsbury's Statutory Instruments*
(3) Lists of Statutory Instruments published in the HMSO cumulative publication lists
(4) Daily List of Government Publications

**Theses**
Index to Theses
Dissertation Abstracts
List of Current Legal Research Topics, Institute of Advanced Legal Studies, University of London

**Words and Phrases**
Beaton's *Scots Law Terms and Expressions*, W. Green, 1982
Broom's *Legal Maxims and Latin Phrases*, 4th ed., Caledonian Books, 1986
The words and phrases sections of *Current Law*
The indexes to law reports
*Stair Memorial Encyclopaedia* contains a glossary of legal terms.